VULCAN

Titles in the *Super Profile* series:

BSA Bantam (F333)
MV Agusta America (F334)
Norton Commando (F335)
Honda CB750 sohc (F351)
Sunbeam S7 & S8 (F363)
BMW R69 & R69S (F387)

Austin-Healey 'Frogeye' Sprite (F343)
Ferrari 250GTO (F308)
Fiat X1/9 (F341)
Ford GT40 (F332)
Jaguar E-Type (F370)
Jaguar D-Type & XKSS (F371)
Jaguar Mk 2 Saloons (F307)

Lotus Elan (F330)
MGB (F305)
MG Midget & Austin-Healey Sprite
(except 'Frogeye') (F344)
Morris Minor & 1000 (ohv) (F331)
Porsche 911 Carrera (F311)
Triumph Stag (F342)

Avro Vulcan (F436)
B29 Superfortress (F339)
Boeing 707 (F356)
de Havilland Mosquito (F422)
Harrier (F357)
Mikoyan-Gurevitch MiG 21 (F439)

P51 Mustang (F423)
Phantom II (F376)
Sea King (F377)
SEPECAT Jaguar (F438)
Super Etendard (F378)
Tiger Moth (F421)
Bell UH-1 Iroquois (F437)

Deltics (F430)
Great Western Kings (F426)
Green Arrow (F427)
Gresley Pacifics (F429)
InterCity 125 (F428)
Royal Scot (F431)

ISBN 0 85429 451 1

A **FOULIS** Aircraft Book

First published 1984

© 1984 **Winchmore Publishing Services Limited**

Published by:
Haynes Publishing Group
Sparkford, Yeovil,
Somerset BA22 7JJ

Distributed in USA by:
Haynes Publications Inc.
861 Lawrence Drive,
Newbury Park,
California 91320, USA

Produced by:
Winchmore Publishing Services Limited,
40 Triton Square,
London NW1 3HG

Printed in Yugoslavia by Mladinska Knjiga

Chant, Christopher
    AVRO Vulcan super profile.—(Super profile)
    1. Vulcan (Jet bomber)
    I. Title   II. Series
    623.74'63   UG1242.B6

    ISBN 0-85429-436-8

Further titles in this series will be published at regular
intervals. For information on new titles please contact
your bookseller or write to the publisher.

Contents

Genesis   4

Type 698 Prototypes and Type 707   26

The Vulcan B.Mk 1   37

The Vulcan B.Mk 2   43

The Ultimate Developments   55

Genesis

The end of World War II left the United Kingdom in an extraordinarily difficult position: victorious in the Allied war against Germany, Italy and Japan, she had immensely strong armed forces of high numerical strength and great technological capability. Yet the American use of two atomic bombs against Japan in August 1945 had at a stroke rendered these forces all but obsolete: the conventional wisdom of the era swayed strongly to the opinion that future wars must of necessity be nuclear. Thus the British armed forces were seen to be of limited value in their current state, while the crippling expense of just under six years of devastating warfare had reduced the country's economy to a state where massive capital expenditure on wholly new projects was all but impossible.

The situation did not seem completely lost, however, for the country was working very closely with the USA, in the development of whose atomic weapons British scientists had played a major role. Given this access to nuclear technology, the country's leaders felt that it was not an insurmountable problem to develop with indigenous resources (working on the mass of German experimental data captured at the end of the war) an aircraft capable of delivering the atomic bombs of the period.

Where the leadership, both political and military, had erred was in assuming that World War II would be followed by a 'breathing period' comparable to that after World War I. There was growing tension between the USA and USSR, erstwhile partners and now edging towards open confrontation as the superpowers behind the 'cold war'. This tension was largely kept under control, the two most powerful countries on Earth being content to test each other's military and political resolve in a number of clashes generally involving third parties in remoter areas of the world, or in crises such as the Soviet blockade of Berlin in 1948 that led to the Berlin Airlift and ultimately to the formation of the North Atlantic Treaty Organization alliance. But though war between the superpowers did not break out, both sides had to arm against such a contingency. The result was an expensive and far-reaching research and development programme on each side of the 'iron curtain', resulting amongst other things in the rapid evolution of new generations of combat aircraft that soon rendered obsolete even those aircraft produced right at the end of World War II.

The prototype Vulcan (VX 770) shows off the almost pure delta planform of the vast wing. Note the crinkling in the skinning of the wing centre section.

For political and economic reasons, there was no doubt in the minds of the Labour administration of the day that the UK was and should remain a world power, with armed forces that must of necessity be able to play a part in such ambitions. This meant that, amongst other things, RAF Bomber Command must be able to deliver nuclear weapons. It was clear that the massive area-bombing night force developed in World War II round the Avro Lancaster and Handley Page Halifax was useless for the task: even the advent of the much improved Avro Lincoln could not alter this. The Air Staff quickly appreciated that Bomber Command had to be transmogrified into a weapon of great precision, with relatively small numbers of advanced bombers each able to deliver a decisive blow with an atomic weapon. Added impetus was imposed on the notion by the passing in August 1946 of the McMahon Act in the USA: this ended any chances of continuing the previous co-operation in nuclear technology by forbidding the passing-on of any US nuclear information to another country.

The Labour government of Clement Attlee at this stage refused to commit itself to the production of an independent British nuclear weapon, but did set in motion the development programme that would permit the rapid evolution of such a weapon should the occasion demand. In the two years after the end of World War II the UK thus saw the establishment of an experimental nuclear establishment at Harwell, production reactors at Windscale and a low-separation diffusion plant at Capenhurst, all based on the secure availability of uranium ore from the Belgian Congo and other sources.

The eventual decision to develop an all-British nuclear weapon was taken early in 1947. At this time the concept of deterrence was ill-defined (indeed, had hardly been born), the British government's decision being based upon the need to develop a weapon that could (and in certain cases would) be used in pursuit of the ideal of restoring the UK to its rightful position of prominence on the world stage.

At this stage the Air Staff was one step ahead of the government, for it had decided to work towards the development of an aircraft capable of delivering a nuclear weapon even before the government had decided to produce such a 'special store', the contemporary euphemism for an atomic bomb of the free-fall type. The Air Staff, under the able leadership of Marshal of the Royal Air Force the Viscount Tedder, had come to the inevitable but courageous decision that the UK could not in the future indulge in a war of attrition (such as that from which it had just staggered), but must be prepared in any future conflict to strike a series of decisive blows right at the outset. In Tedder's words, the Royal Air Force in peacetime must become a 'full-grown David' rather than the 'embryo Goliath' that it had been in the 1930s. The cornerstones of warfare in the new nuclear age, the Air Staff concluded, must be extreme mobility and massive firepower in the hands of small but immensely skilled crews operating advanced aircraft.

This then was the political and military background against which was developed Specification B.35/46, worked out during 1946 and issued in January 1947 before the government had made its decision to develop the British 'bomb'. The specification was extraordinarily difficult, and by the standards of the day impossible to meet. The Air Staff must have appreciated the fact, but issued the specification almost as a challenge to the British aircraft industry, which had performed design wonders in World War II, and was now avidly absorbing the fruits of

German aeronautical (principally aerodynamic) research during that war. The requirement called for a bomber with a crew of five (in pressurized accommodation) able to carry a 10,000-lb (4,536-kg) 'special store' at speeds in the order of 575 mph (925 km/h) to a target some 1,725 miles (2,776 km) distant; still-air range was to be in the order of 3,860 miles (6,212 km). So far so good, for the specification, though taxing, was not hopelessly unrealistic given the new generation of jet engines under development for marriage to an advanced airframe making full use of the German research material. The real difficulty lay in combining the structural and aerodynamic features that would make possible these performance parameters in an airframe with a maximum take-off weight of only 100,000 lb (45,360 kg) and possessing an internal bomb bay able to accommodate a 'special store' measuring 25 ft (7.62 m) in length and 5 ft (1.52 m) in diameter or an alternative load of 20 1,000-lb (454-kg) conventional bombs over a shorter range; a jettisonable cabin pressurized to 9 lb/sq in (0.62 bar), offering the equivalent of 8,000 ft (2,440 m) at a cruising altitude of 45,000 ft (13,715 m), reducable to 3.5 lb/sq in (0.24 bar) over the target to reduce the hazards of explosive decompression should the cabin be hit by shell splinters; a ceiling increasing to 50,000 ft (15,240 m) over the target with fuel burn; features such as an advanced radar (based on the wartime H2S) for navigation and bombing, though a visual bombing capability was also to be retained, despite the problems it posed for the design of the cabin; and a landing speed of not more than 120 mph (193 km/h). The specification was phenomenally exacting: the requirements could all be met, but the range, ceiling and landing speeds all called for a large wing, and this could not be envisaged within the limitation of a

KEY TO DRAWING

 1 Dielectric nose 13ft x 8ft
 2 Flight Refuelling probe
 3 Radar scanner
 4 Vent; cabin air discharge into bay
 5 Front pressure bulkhead
 6 Access hatch to nose
 7 Rear pressure bulkhead, nosewheel beams on rear face
 8 Jettisonable canopy
 9 Production breaks
 10 Pilot, co-pilot, Martin-Baker Mk 4 ejection seats
 11 Flying-control assembly, toe brakes
 12 Flying-control push-pull tubes
 13 Feel-simulator input
 14 Engine control-runs
 15 Three non-ejecting seats, signaller, master-nav./air-bomber, second navigator
 16 Working desk
 17 Radio and radar racks
 18 Ladder to pilots' deck
 19 Visual air-bomber's prone position
 20 Bomb-sight
 21 Crew entry and lower-deck escape-hatch
 22 Pneumatic actuating jacks
 23 Ladder, ground equipment
 24 Dinghy stowage in canopy fairing
 25 Periscopes each side, external inspection
 26 Ground rescue equipment; destructor to starboard
 27 Cabin pressure and air-conditioning pack
 28 Intake to 27 (starboard intake to 37)
 29 Intercooler and turbine exhaust
 30 Cabin-air feed and extractor duct
 31 Dowty liquid spring, levered-suspension nosewheel unit
 32 Magnesium-alloy casting
 33 Breaker strut

 65 Rotax generator in nose-bullet (all engines)
 66 Accessory group, pumps, fuel-cooled oil cooler
 67 Engine mounting points
 68 Compressor bleed ducts, anti-icing, cabin air
 69 Firewalls
 70 Fire-shrouds
 71 "Alfol" covered jet pipes (app. 22 ft long)
 72 Jet-pipe heat shroud
 73 Engine access doors
 74 Cool air to engine bays
 75 Warren truss rib between jet pipes
 76 Jet-pipe rail
 77 Jet-pipe nozzle area adjusters
 78 Dowty liquid spring bogie under-carriage
 79 Shock absorber
 80 Braking drag strut
 81 Mainwheel retraction jack
 82 Pivot points in wing structure
 83 Internal light
 84 Dunlop tyres, wheels and (Maxaret) brakes
 85 Door linked to leg
 86 Wheel-bay door jacks
 87 Camera bay
 88 Front spar/leading-edge units
 89 Rear spar/trailing-edge units
 90 Skin "planks," stringers attached
 91 Drooped leading edge
 92 Thermal anti-icing ducts
 93 Corrugated inner skin

 34 Jack (4,000 lb/sq in system)
 35 Steering cylinder (internal final drive) ±47.5 deg
 36 Nosewheel door jacks
 37 Equipment bay, hydraulics, pneumatics, electrics, electronics
 38 Inverters (three)
 39 Cooling air to 38
 40 Boundary-layer bleed 'fence'
 41 Boundary-layer duct and outlet
 42 Three-position air brakes
 43 Cam-track (brake surface angle)
 44 Sprocket and chain drive, central motor
 45 Roller guides
 46 Weapons-bay door actuating cylinder
 47 Concertina type doors
 48 Subsidiary stores bay
 49 Electrics bay
 50 Access to 49
 51 Five batteries
 52 Vertical stiffeners on rear spar for fin loads
 53 Rudder power control (Boulton Paul duplicated electric/hydraulic pack)
 54 Cooling-air in
 55 Cooling-air out
 56 Access to 53
 57 Tail bumper
 58 Braking parachute box (starboard)
 59 Streaming point for drag 'chute
 60 Dielectric tail cone
 61 Bifurcated engine-air intake
 62 Engine air ducts through front spar
 63 Detachable duct section
 64 Bristol Olympus two-spool engines (11,000 to 13,000 lb thrust)

 94 Elevators
 95 Ailerons
 96 Power-control jacks (see 53)
 97 Irving-type pressure-sealed balance (and mass balance)
 98 Hinges on upper surface
 99 Honeycomb sandwich inspection panels
100 Landing lamps
101 Pressure refuelling points
102 Navigation lights
103 Glide/slope aerial
104 Gee aerial

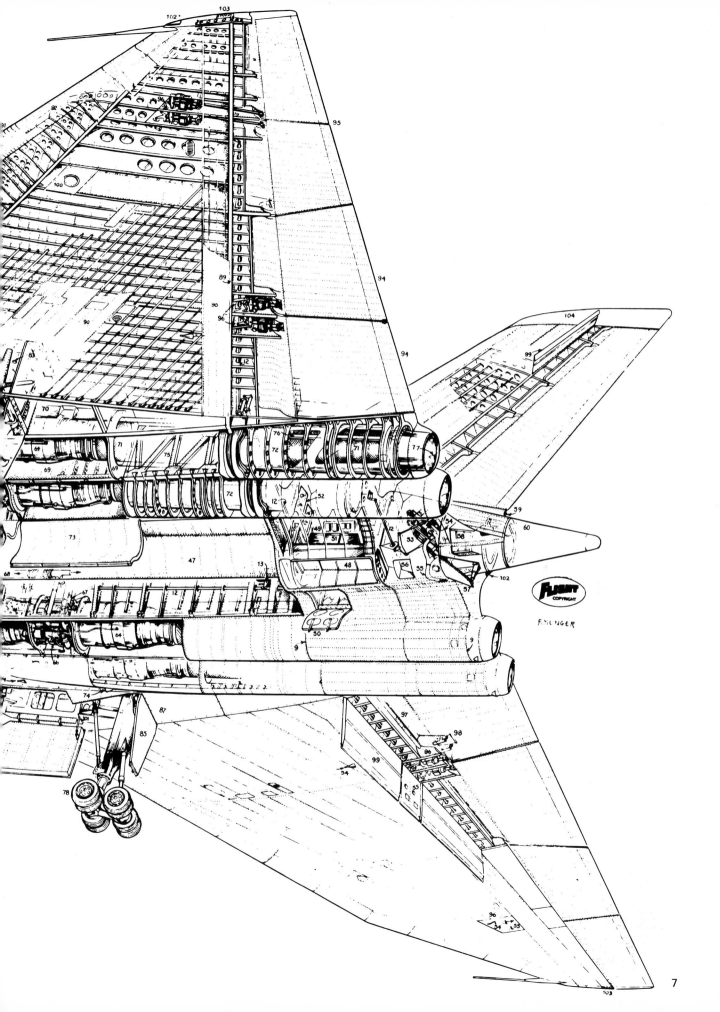

7

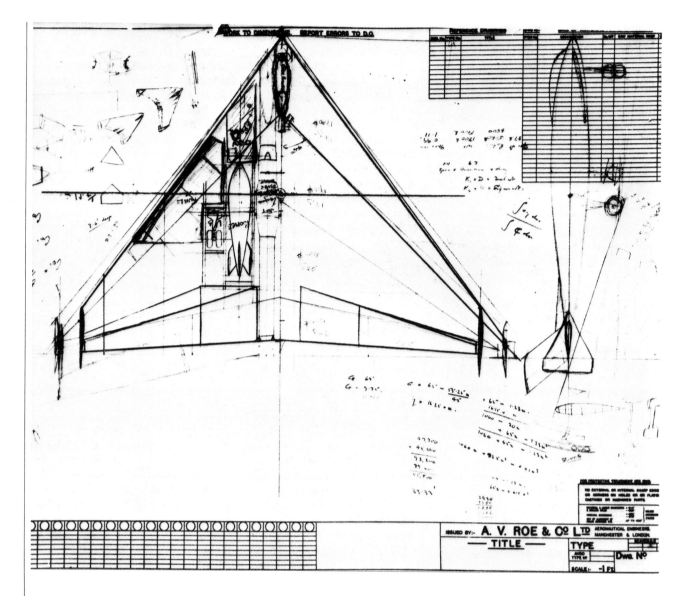

Inside the drawing title block:
WORK TO DIMENSIONS. REPORT ERRORS TO D.O.

ISSUED BY:- A. V. ROE & Co LTD AERONAUTICAL ENGINEERS. MANCHESTER & LONDON.
— TITLE —   TYPE
AVRO TYPE No   Dwg. No
SCALE:- =1 FT.

A preliminary sketch for the Type 698 reveals the outboard vertical surfaces, superimposed engines and offset bomb stowage.

100,000-lb (45,360-kg) maximum take-off weight. How or why the Air Staff arrived at this figure has never been revealed, but it placed the whole programme in jeopardy even before it had been issued. But creativity in the airframe business was high, spurred on by the desire to regain orders cut back with the end of hostilities in 1945, and eight companies tendered to the demands of Specification B.35/46: these were Armstrong Whitworth, Avro (A. V. Roe Ltd), Blackburn, Bristol, English Electric, Handley Page, Short and Vickers. Blackburn, Bristol and English Electric were soon eliminated from the competition, and the Ministry

of Supply finally opted for the designs from Avro and Handley Page, the two companies which had dominated heavy bomber design for RAF Bomber Command in World War II.

The Air Staff was fully aware of the difficulties imposed by its specification, and in August 1947 issued another and less demanding requirement, Specification B.14/46. This had been drafted before B.35/46, and was now issued to provide the RAF with the possibility of a less advanced but still capable aircraft should the B.35/46 aircraft be seriously delayed, as was increasingly likely to be the case.

Specification B.14/46 called for a straight-wing aircraft with the same range and payload requirements as the Specification B.35/46 aircraft, but a ceiling of 45,000 ft (13,715 m) and a speed of only 450 mph (724 km/h). The solution to this requirement finally emerged as the highly capable Short SA4 Sperrin, a most interesting design with four jet engines in superimposed pairs on each wing. This excellent machine did not reach production for a number of reasons, so the ball was back in the court of the Specification B.35/46 contenders. A tender-design conference on 28 July 1947 confirmed the Ministry of Supply's decision to proceed with the Avro and Handley Page submissions to Specification B.35/46, as noted above. Intention-to-proceed notifications were awarded on 19 November to Handley Page for its H.P.80 submission, which finally emerged as the Victor 'crescent-wing' bomber, and 1 January 1948 to Avro for its Avro Type 698 submission, which finally emerged as the Vulcan delta-wing bomber.

There were already serious problems with the anticipated gestation times for these programmes, however, and it was decided additionally to press ahead with the design and production of the Vickers Type 660, a less ambitious contender which had earlier been knocked from the running. This moderately swept design was enshrined in Specification B.9/48, which was issued on 19 July 1948, some three months after Vickers had been informed of the Ministry's intention to proceed with two prototypes of what finally entered service as the first of the UK's three V-bombers, the Valiant.

The design of the Avro Type 698 was headed by the company's technical director Roy Chadwick, who had been responsible for a number of important aircraft such as the wartime Lancaster and Lincoln, and the post-war Tudor Airliner. Chadwick and his team soon found that the requirements of Specification B.35/46 were monumentally difficult to reconcile with the maximum weight specified: early design studies showed that the performance figures could almost (but definitely not) be met by a 'conventional' design with 45° swept flying surfaces, but only at a maximum take-off weight of 195,000 lb (88,452 kg), almost double what the Air Staff had imposed. The

design team was fully aware of the difficulties: the in-service Boeing B-29 carried much the same payload as the specified design, but had entered service with a maximum take-off weight of 135,000 lb (61,236 kg) and offered much inferior performance, and it is worth noting that in Specification B.14/46 the Air Staff would shortly call for a less capable aircraft that could carry the same bombload over the same range after a take-off at a maximum weight of 140,000 lb (63,504 kg), though a weight of 120,000 lb (54,432 kg) was preferred 'if attainable'.

It was fairly clear, therefore, that the Air Staff's weight limit was impossible, but its demands had the excellent effect of 'concentrating the mind wonderfully' for the design team. Although contemporary Avro projects such as the updated Anson trainer, the Tudor airliner, the Athena trainer and the Shackleton maritime reconnaissance aircraft were already occupying the company and its senior design personnel, the Type 698 project was entrusted to an extremely competent team headed by Chadwick, with Stuart 'Cock' Davies as chief designer, Eric Priestly (later Roy Ewans) as chief aerodynamicist and J. G. Willis (later Gilbert Whitehead) as project engineer.

Thus the 45° sweep concept could be used only as a starting point: wing structure weight had increased considerably as a result of the reduction of thickness/chord ratio from some 23 per cent used on wartime Avro aircraft to 12 per cent to meet speed requirements as laid down in Specification B.35/46, and it was clear that while a lightening of the structure could be achieved by thickening the wing, this would have adverse results on speed, which was already below that specified.

In its efforts to reduce all-up weight, the Avro team was thus forced to look at radical methods

for reducing structure weight, and by early February 1947 it had begun to consider a tailless design, which would benefit from the elimination of the horizontal tail (vertical surfaces had to be retained for directional control) and rear fuselage. There had been considerable interest in such types both during and after World War II, and at the beginning of 1947 there were some 15 or more tailless designs in the air. Great interest had been shown in German designs such as the Messerschmitt Me 163 fighter and Horten-designed Gotha 229, and already flying in the UK were the de Havilland D.H.108 and Armstrong Whitworth A.W.52. Of the British designs, the former was a tailless development of the Vampire fighter, and the latter a jet-powered development of the A.W.52G tailless research glider. But Chadwick and his team thought that greater possibilities were offered by the tailless designs of John Northrop in the USA, namely the XB-35 piston-engined heavy bomber and its YB-49 jet-powered derivative. These were impressively clean aircraft in the aerodynamic sense, and offered extremely high performance and good load-carrying capability with only modest engine power. Examples of both types had been lost in the air, but it was clear that both aerodynamically and structurally the tailless design was fully practical for a large aircraft.

The Avro design was therefore recast as a flying wing, retaining the 45° sweep of its forebear, wingtip elevons in place of ailerons conferring adequate control in pitch and roll axes, and small tip-mounted vertical surfaces being adequate for control in the yaw axis. Chadwick, impressed with the tandem main landing gear arrangement of the Boeing XB-47 and Martin XB-48 prototype bombers for the USAAF, suggested a similar arrangement, with small outriggered wheels for

Above: Though wing shape and other features were altered in late-production aircraft, the dominating impression was still the vast wing area of the graceful Vulcan.
Left: A Vulcan B.Mk 2A of RAF Strike Command's No. 44 Squadron shows off its paces.

Below: Despite the addition of fin packages, inflight-refuelling probe and terrain-following radar radome, the Vulcan's head-on aspect is controlled by the vast inlets and deep wing.

Designed for the carriage of nuclear or
conventional free-fall weapons, the Vulcan as
finally produced had a cavernous bomb bay
on the centre of gravity between the two
pairs of engines.

lateral stability, and the recast machine weighed in at some 137,000 lb (62,143 kg) thanks to reduced structure weight, reduced drag and therefore reduced fuel requirement.

This was clearly much closer to a definitive project, but it was also a radical solution to the Air Staff requirement, and had thus to be very carefully considered for flaws. Chadwick's main worry centred on the problems that might be associated with the shift of the centre of gravity as fuel was burned and the bombs dropped. He considered that this might cause severe control problems, and this also raised again the possibility of reducing structure weight, which was still high as a result of the use of a relatively thin wing of high aspect ratio. Clearly an increased thickness/chord ratio would ease structural problems

and permit a lighter wing, but this would reduce speed. The solution appeared to lie with a considerable increase in root chord by 'filling in' the area behind the trailing edge to produce a 'delta-wing' aircraft, with total area little altered from that of the swept-wing tailless design but aspect ratio lowered to about 2.4. This permitted the use of a very thick wing which still had a relatively low thickness/chord ratio, so that structural and performance criteria were met at the same time.

Thus March 1947 may be regarded as the decisive point in the evolution of the Vulcan, for the team had arrived at the triangular delta wing that went most of the way to meeting Chadwick's ideal of a true flying wing, and also offered light weight and high performance with the added bonuses of considerable internal

volume for the landing gear, powerplant, fuel, payload and crew. Chadwick's team also appreciated that the previously anticipated problems with centre-of-gravity shift had disappeared, and that the large wing offered the possibility of high ceiling and low approach speed.

However, this refined design was still further from the mainstream of aeronautical development than its predecessor, and so radical a design had to be very carefully considered before being tendered officially. During March and April 1947 the concept was honed towards perfection, and was finally offered in May

Below: Compared with that of modern aircraft, the Vulcan's first pilot had a relatively simple instrument panel.
Below right: The second pilot's panel was only slightly different.

1947 as the Avro Type 698. This was an almost pure delta aircraft, the vestigial nose accommodating the pressure cabin for the five crewmen and being blended carefully into the centre section of the vast wing, whose lines were broken in planform only by the engine inlets and exhausts. The three engine types available were the Bristol BE.10, the Metrovick F.9 and the Rolls-Royce AJ.65, all offering some 9,000 lb (4,082 kg) of thrust. The Avro team opted for the Bristol engine, disposed in a somewhat unique configuration: the two engines in each wing were aligned as a superimposed pair, the upper engine forward of the lower engine and exhausting through a nozzle in the upper surface of the wing at about 70 per cent chord; the lower engine exhausted through a jetpipe emerging through a cutout in the

inner part of the trailing edge. Each pair of engines was to be fed by a large circular inlet in the leading edge just outboard of the crew nacelle. The rump of the 'fuselage' ended just aft of the trailing edge in a radome for the rear-warning radar. Other notable external features were the sharply-swept twin vertical tail surfaces, each with an inset rudder, just outboard of the two elevons that occupied most of the trailing edge outboard of the jetpipes, and the twin-wheel bogies on the tricycle landing gear, of which the main units retracted forward into wing bays outboard of the engines and the nose unit into the fuselage aft of the cabin. Where the bomb bay might have been expected, along the centreline, was fuel and volume for the aircraft's extensive systems. Payload was thus located in a wing bay just outboard of the port

engines, with balancing fuel in a comparable bay in the starboard wing; if a conventional bombload was specified, plans called for this to be carried half in each wing bay, with a consequent reduction in fuel capacity.

This then was the Avro Type 698 submitted to the Air Ministry in May 1947. Such was the esteem in which Chadwick was held at the time that the project was not rejected, and Chadwick attended frequent meetings to urge on his company's proposal. In one of those tragic accidents that mar so many fields of endeavour, Chadwick was killed on 23 August 1947 when an Avro Tudor in which he was making a test flight crashed because the ailerons cables had been connected the wrong way round. Chadwick was succeeded as technical director by W. S. Farren, also a highly capable

Below and behind the two pilots were the other three members of the Vulcan's crew, each seated on a standard bucket seat (non-ejecting) facing the rear bulkhead of the cockpit section. Each man had a seat dinghy, and a Type H dinghy was stowed in the rear of the canopy. For rapid escape these three crew members had to use the undernose access door, actuated in emergencies by a rear-cockpit handle to extend into the vertical position as a windbreak.

Left: On the left of the lower compartment sat the radar operator.

Below: On the right was located the air electronics officer.

designer, and the Type 698 survived the death of its father.

But although, as related above, the Type 698 proposal was accepted by the Air Ministry on 27 November 1947, the design was still destined to undergo a great deal of development, largely as a result of the representations of the Royal Aircraft Establishment at Farnborough, where the design had undergone a complete technical critique. Farnborough's suggestion was that Avro had 'got its sums wrong' about the Type 698's high subsonic cruise speed, and that this could be obtained only by using a thinner wing. Avro conceded the fact and again set to work recasting the

Type 698 design with a thinner wing. This in turn entailed a host of other alterations, and while the revised aircraft bore a marked similarity to its predecessor, it had a number of major differences. The engines could no longer be located as a superimposed pair in each wing, which now lacked the depth for such an installation, so they were placed as side-by-side pairs, still fed by unaltered circular inlets but now exhausting from jetpipes that projected slightly aft of the trailing edge. The revised wing also lacked the depth for the previous payload/fuel arrangement of symmetrical bays, but the solution was easily found in the provision of a larger and more conventional fuselage accommodating a large bomb bay on the centre-of-gravity position. The fuel was shifted out to the wings, which were just thick enough to accommodate

unaltered main landing gear units. Control had been under investigation for some time, and the revised aircraft underwent a series of interesting design modifications in this field. The first suggestion was the incorporation of the double tandem elevons pioneered with great success on the A.W.52 flying wing research aircraft; then, in March 1948, the Avro design team decided to apply information just available on the use of pivoting wingtips, whose actuators and drives necessitated the inward movement of the vertical tail surfaces. Finally, in September 1948, the design arrived at its definitive control arrangement, with the whole of the trailing edge given over to separate ailerons (outboard) and elevators (inboard). This meant that the vertical tail surfaces had to be removed, the solution being found in the use of a conventional

Below: A legacy from an earlier era was the incorporation of sextant positions, this being the starboard station.
Below right: The port sextant position.

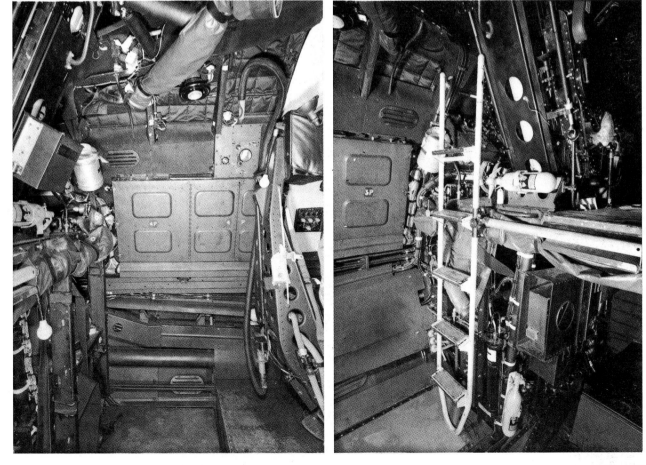

single fin and large trailing rudder on the fuselage centreline. This also placated the critics who foresaw longitudinal control problems, for if necessary the fin could become the support for a high-set tailplane. Of the design team, Ewans was particularly pleased with the use of this large fin-and-rudder assembly, for he had been concerned about the original Type 698's potential problems at high angles of attack at low airspeeds, and also at high airspeeds at high altitude. The final revision led to the replacement of the circular inlets by long horizontal slots in an extended wing leading edge (advocated by Farnborough) on each side of the fuselage, which had a larger nose than previously, and accommodated a large navigation/bombing radar and a pressurized cabin for the five crew. Only the pilot and co-pilot were provided with ejector seats, the previous demand for a jettisonable crew compartment having been abandoned some time earlier as wholly unworkable.

The intention-to-proceed notification of 1 January 1948 was confirmed on 28 July 1948 when the Ministry of Supply formally contracted with Avro for the production of two Type 698 prototypes (VX770 and VX777) from the Chadderton factory between Manchester and Oldham, with test flying to be started at the company's nearby airfield at Woodford.

Well displayed along the wing trailing edges of this Vulcan B.Mk 2A are the elevons, each wing having two large inboard surfaces and two small outboard surfaces, each controlled by its own jack.

Right: Seen in the white anti-radiation paint scheme used between 1956 and 1964, XA 903 was the last airworthy Vulcan B.Mk 1, and among its distinctions were carrying trials with the Blue Steel missile, then development flying with the Olympus powerplant for the Concorde supersonic airliner (flying from September 1966 to August 1971) and finally development flying with the RB.199 powerplant for the Panavia Tornado (flying from April 1973 to February 1979).

Below: The Vulcan B.Mk 1 series featured a trailing edge control system of ailerons (outboard) and elevators (inboard).

Delivered as a Vulcan B.Mk 2, XH 534 was later converted to Vulcan B.Mk 2A standard, and is here seen as a Vulcan SR.Mk 2 on patrol over the North Sea in the hands of No. 27 Squadron from RAF Scampton. The squadron badge, on the fin, is a white circle containing a depiction of Dumbo, the flying elephant.

Above: XL 360 was a Vulcan B.Mk 2A, and the pimple on the extreme nose housed the antenna for the terrain-following radar adopted when the Vulcan was switched to the low-level role.

Below: XM 597 was a Vulcan B.Mk 2A on the strength of No. 44 Squadron, RAF Strike Command, and based at RAF Waddington.

Left: A Vulcan B.Mk 2 shows off its massive wing but generally clean appearance.

Above: The pilot of a No. 617 Squadron Vulcan B.Mk 2A lifts the nose of his aircraft before departing the runway, probably at the squadron's home base of RAF Scampton.

Left: Carrying on its fin the badge of the Waddington Wing and the red motif of No. 50 Squadron, this aircraft is revealed as a Vulcan K.Mk 2 tanker by the drogue box under the tailcone.

Right: Sporting the Dumbo motif of No. 27 Squadron on its fin, this Vulcan SR.Mk 2 was tasked with long-range maritime reconnaissance.

Right: A Vulcan B.Mk 2A makes a low-level pass at an air display, where the presence of a Vulcan was always a great draw.

Above: XM 606 was a Vulcan B.Mk 2, and the first of the series to be fitted with terrain-following radar. The type is seen here in low-level camouflage and low-visibility Type B roundels and fin flash (without white). Just visible behind the fuselage roundel is the yellow mouth of the black panther borne by aircraft of No. 1 Group, RAF Strike Command.

Left: XM 597 was the first Vulcan B.Mk 2A fitted with ARI.18228 radar warning on the fin, and was an aircraft of No. 44 Squadron of the Waddington Wing.

XL 320 was a Vulcan B.Mk 2 of No. 230
Operational Conversion Unit, whose fin flash
is clearly evident, and based at RAF
Scampton. The accompanying aircraft is a
Handley Page Hastings.

Above: The Falklands campaign of 1982 brought home to the RAF the problems of its limited inflight-refuelling capability, the force of BAe Victor aircraft being fully extended. In April 1982 BAe and Ministry of Defence talks investigated the possibility of Vulcan tanker conversions, and a go-ahead was issued on 4 May. Just 50 days later the first Vulcan K.Mk 2A conversion was delivered to RAF Waddington, only five days after its first flight on 18 June. Seen here is such a conversion, with the Flight Refuelling Ltd hose drum unit in the erstwhile ECM compartment, with the drogue unit in a metal and wood box under it. Fuel is fed from three tanks in the bomb bay.

Left: Ground crew of No. 50 Squadron service the drogue unit of a Vulcan K.Mk 2A at RAF Waddington.

Above: XM 656 was the penultimate Vulcan production item, and here displays the sturdy landing gear of the Type 698 series.

Below: A camouflaged Vulcan B.Mk 2A of No. 44 Squadron shows off the type's rear view.

Type 698 Prototypes and Type 707

Given the radical nature of the Type 698 design, there had for some time been suggestions that features of it should be tested in small-scale aircraft, the initial proposal being a delta glider that could be towed into the air and released for trials into the Type 698's low-speed handling characteristics. But by 1948 it had been decided that a powered type would offer greater scope for trials, and would enable additional aspects of the flight characteristics to be explored.

The result was the Avro Type 707, which was to have linear dimensions approximately one-third of those of the Type 698. Unfortunately, the Type 707 programme was launched as something of an afterthought, and when the first was ordered by the intention-to-proceed notification for the two Type 698 prototypes in January 1948, it was too late to do anything but run parallel with its larger relation. Nevertheless, the Type 707 programme provided much valuable research and development data, some of which could be applied to the Type 698. The first requirement was for two considerably different aircraft, a Type 707 (VX784) to Specification E.15/48, and an Avro Type 710 (VX790). The Type 707 was a simple aircraft designed to provide a means of evaluating the Type 698's low-speed characteristics. For reasons of economy and speed (both of design and of construction), the Type 707 was kept as simple as possible, and as far as was possible used components from existing aircraft, such as the main landing gear units of the Athena and the cockpit canopy of the Gloster Meteor. The aircraft began to take shape in the summer of 1948 as a trim little delta, its Rolls-Royce Derwent turbojet being

VX 790 was the second Avro 707, more specifically the Type 707B and designed for investigation of the low-speed handling characteristics of the delta.

Streaming its anti-spin parachute, the Avro 707B comes in to land. The dorsal inlet proved a hindrance to trials.

located in the rear fuselage, where it was fed with air from two dorsal inlets and with fuel from a centre-fuselage tank.

VX784 was able to undertake ground handling and taxiing trials at Woodford in August 1949, but was then moved by road to the Aircraft and Armament Experimental Establishment at Boscombe Down in Wiltshire for flight trials. The first flight was made by an Avro pilot, Flight Lieutenant Eric Esler, on 6 September, and was uneventful, the Type 707 proving itself to have unexceptional handling characteristics in the air. After a few more test flights the Type 707 was flown to Farnborough to participate in that year's Society of British Aircraft Constructors' display – where the unique configuration of the machine made a considerable impact – and then returned to Boscombe Down for the installation of test equipment. In the last week of September 1949 all was ready for the start of instrumented trials but, for reasons which have never been fully resolved, the Type 707 crashed near Blackbushe. Esler was killed in this disaster, possibly because the type was not fitted with an ejector seat.

Meanwhile Avro had been pushing ahead with the design of the Type 710, which was an altogether more ambitious design intended to validate the Type 698's high-speed handling characteristics. The proposed powerplant was a pair of Rolls-Royce Avon turbojets, but it was soon appreciated that the effort devoted to the Type 710 was curtailing development of the Type 698, and that the whole programme would be seriously delayed if the Type 698 had to be held back to incorporate lessons learned from the flight trials of the Type 710, which could not possibly take place until the early 1950s. It was decided to abandon the Type 710, and also a full-scale but simplified Type 698, which could be airborne after a relatively short period of development, in favour of an expanded Type 707 programme.

With the cancellation of the Type 710, therefore, the serial VX790 was reallocated to a second Type 707, designated Avro Type 707B. This was similar to its predecessor, but had revised elevators and air brakes, and was fitted with the nose section of the Type 707A (see below) complete with an ejector seat. Another alteration concerned the nosewheel: in the Type 707 this had come from a Meteor, but in the Type 707B it came from the Hawker P.1052 research aircraft.

The new aircraft was completed in August 1950 and was trucked to Boscombe Down before any runway trials had been made. The Type 707B was ready for flight late on 5 September 1950, and in the hands of Wing Commander R. J. 'Roly' Falk the aircraft made a short hop in the evening dusk before recording its official first flight on the following day. Falk was absolutely delighted with the type's excellent handling, and immediately secured permission from Avro and the Air Ministry to fly to Farnborough to take part in that year's SBAC display. The aircraft arrived on the first day, offering the crowd a superb contrast in scale as it circled to permit the vast Bristol Brabazon to lift off the runway before it touched down.

Immediately after the SBAC display the Type 707B was prepared for instrumented flight trials in the speed range from 92 to 403 mph (148 to 649 km/h). These proved very valuable, though their relevance to the Type 698 programme was limited, largely because of the Type 707B's lack of powered controls and use of dorsal inlets. Nevertheless, the Type 707B did contribute somewhat to the development of the Type 698, the most notable contribution being the realization as a result of the test programme that the jetpipes for the BE.10

Designed as a dual-control trainer, the sole Avro 707C was used mainly for research into powered controls and electronics.

engines of the Type 698 should be angled downwards to mitigate the effects on longitudinal stability and trim of different power settings. Trials with the Type 707B also confirmed that a longer nosewheel leg was desirable (that of the Type 707B was lengthened by 9 in/ 22.86 cm) to increase the wing's angle of incidence and so shorten the take-off run required. The Type 707B was flown for about 100 hours in support of the Type 698 programme, and after this effort at Woodford in 1951 was sent to Boscombe Down for further trials in 1952.

While this small-scale programme had been gathering pace, that of the full-size Type 698 had been slowed for two reasons: Avro's lack of drawing office area at a time that the Shackleton maritime reconnaissance aircraft was coming to fruition, and the desire not to press ahead too quickly before the results of

another research programme became available. This other programme concerned the Type 698's high-speed handling characteristics, which were to be explored using the Avro Type 707A research aircraft. This aircraft was ordered to Specification E.10/49 in 1950, and incorporated many of the Royal Aircraft Establishment's recommendations about the design of the Type 698's wing. The result was an aircraft modelled far more closely on the Type 698, with ailerons and elevators to scale (and fitted with servo tabs to simulate the Type 698's powered controls), a revised forward fuselage of finer lines than that used on the Type 707, and wing-root inlets. The Type 707A was serialled WD280 and first flew, with Falk at the controls, on 14 July 1951. The machine undertook some 92 hours of tests before May 1952, and contributed fairly considerably to the ultimate development of the Type 698. In 1956 it was shipped to Australia for further trials of an aerodynamic

nature, and is now preserved in Melbourne.

Production of the Type 707 series comprised just another two aircraft, although at the time it was supposed that it might be more. The first of these was another Type 707A (WZ736), all but identical with the original Type 707A and used by the Royal Aircraft Establishment for the development of automatic throttles until its retirement in 1967 to the museum at RAF Finningley. The second machine was the only Avro Type 707C, a side-by-side two-seat trainer serialled WZ744. This had been proposed as the first of a small number of delta trainers, but in the event only the single example was built. The machine was again allocated to the Royal Aircraft Establishment, which used the type for avionics development until it too was retired to Finningley in 1967. The Type 707C had first flown on 1 July 1953.

Back in the Manchester area, the components of the Type 698 prototypes had meanwhile been taking shape. Mentioned here

should be the two main component suppliers who made the greatest contributions to the entire programme. These were Dowty and Boulton Paul, the latter later becoming part of the Dowty group. Starting in 1949, Dowty designed the landing gear for the Type 698. Each unit was a large magnesium alloy casting. The nosewheel unit was fitted with a two-wheel bogie, while each of the main units supported a beam-type bogie pivoted on the leading axle to prevent 'slam' as the heavy aircraft touched down. Each bogie had two axles, each with four wheels. Shock absorption was by Dowty Liquid Spring type with a working pressure of 31,500 lb/sq in (2,171.86 bar). Dowty was responsible for the entire landing gear arrangement, including the massive well doors that held the retracted landing gear in position without the need for uplocks. Actuation was hydraulic, and here Dowty worked hand-in-hand with Boulton Paul, a pioneer of hydraulics for aircraft. Apart from the landing gear actuation system,

Boulton Paul provided the hydraulics for the powered controls. Each of the wing controls (comprising, on each wing, outboard ailerons and inboard elevators, each divided into two equal portions) had its own duplicated system made up of an electric motor, three-bank hydraulic pump and linear actuator. The system for the single-piece rudder was similar, with automatic changeover to the auxiliary system in the event of a main-system failure. All the controls had artificial 'feel', a different type of system being used for each of the three sets of controls. The rudder had the least complex system, with rudder pedal force proportional to the cube of the indicated air speed. More complex were the systems for the elevators and ailerons: the elevators had a normal q-feel system proportional to the square of the indicated air speed, and the ailerons used spring feel within moving limits which were set by stops positioned by a q-feel system. All this was advanced for

its day, but after trials with the Type 698 prototypes the system was gradually evolved further, so that by the time the aircraft began to enter service in 1957 the entire system featured an advanced autostabilization circuit incorporating a Mach trimmer and yaw damper.

The airframe itself was relatively conventional, and built largely of aluminium alloy. The centre of the entire aircraft, both structurally and aerodynamically, was the centre section/centre fuselage portion, which was a box measuring some 51 ft (15.54 m) in length and 27 ft (8.23 m) in width. In the middle of this portion, on the underside, was the large bomb bay, which had two double-folding concertina doors, with strong arches over the top of it to support the inner portions of the wing, namely the engine bays in each wing root. Each of these bays comprised three massive ribs and

29

two widely-spaced main spars, plus a number of bridge girders and lesser structural components. To this structural core were appended the nose section, intermediate and outer wing panels, and the tail section complete with fin and rudder assembly. Fuel was accommodated in the intermediate wing portions (three spanwise tanks inboard and two spanwise tanks outboard), and in fuselage tanks located between the bomb bay and the flight deck. The considerable internal volume of the airframe made the installation of adequate fuel a simple matter, the prime considerations in the location of the fuel cells being the reduction of combat damage likelihood, and the need to maintain longitudinal trim as the fuel was burned. Wide location of the fuel cells provided the solution to the former consideration, while progressive sampling of each of the 14 fuel

cells (10 in the wings and four in the fuselage) maintained the centre of gravity in the optimum position.

The part of the design that gave the Avro team the greatest difficulty was the inner portion of each wing, containing the inlet, twin engine bays and twin jetpipes. By May 1948 the Royal Aircraft Establishment's researches had begun to show that moderately swept inboard wing sections suffered a sharp drag rise at about Mach 0.9, and by the end of 1949 Avro reluctantly agreed that the root leading edges would have to be redefined virtually into a wedge, with the line of maximum thickness pulled forward sharply almost to the leading edge. This in turn required a redesign of the air brakes, which were located above and below the inlet ducts forward of the engines. The brakes finally adopted were simple in design and operation, and appeared to be

wholly inadequate for the task in hand: each wing was intended to have four brakes (two above the wing and two below it), each brake comprising a sandwich panel that lay flat in the surface of the wing until required, when it was pushed well through the boundary layer and turned to an angle of 45° or 90° to the airflow. A single centreline actuator was sufficient to operate all eight brakes which, when turned to the 90° position, increased drag by a prodigious 250 per cent. On production aircraft the outer underwing brakes were omitted. Further braking assistance was provided by a parachute with a diameter of 24 ft (7.32 m). On the prototypes and early production aircraft this was stowed in a box in the

A special rig was built at Woodford for the static testing of a Vulcan airframe. Note the forward pressure bulkhead and area for the radome.

Each of the compact main landing gear units featured an eight-wheel bogie with the beam pivoted on the front axle to avoid 'slamming'.

starboard side of the tailcone, while on later aircraft it was relocated to a fairing on the tailcone aft of the rudder.

The engine bays were particularly large in volume, for the designers were fully aware that though the BE.10 engine (later named Olympus) was the engine they wanted, the development timescale of this advanced engine might well require the use of an alternative. The bays were thus designed with this in mind, and the feature also allowed the subsequent up-engining of the series without undue difficulty. As late as 1950 it was not clear what the ultimate engines would be, but it was apparent that the BE.10 would not be available by the time the first Type 698 was ready for flight. The Avro team considered a host of alternative engines and installations, including six-engine powerplants with three engines on each side of a widened centre section or with the two additional engines in pods under the wings, but finally decided on the Rolls-Royce Avon RA.3, rated at 6,500-lb (2,948-kg) thrust. As may be imagined, this was a marginal powerplant for so large an aircraft, despite the fact that the first prototype was completed without provision for wing fuel, pressurization, military equipment and a number of other items including a seat for the co-pilot. Production of the Type 698 prototypes had begun in 1951, and at the end of the year the various portions had been moved to Woodford for construction. The choice of engine was the final decision to be made, and assembly of VX770 began early in 1952, the Avro team's spur being the need to beat Handley Page's H.P.80 into the air, preferably in time for the 1952 SBAC display.

All along it had been the intention of the Air Ministry to order one of these two main contenders as the principal aircraft of the UK's new strategic bombing force, but such were the exigencies of a rapidly deteriorating world situation in the early 1950s, with the Korean War raging, the superpowers locked in bitter political confrontation, and the impotence of the UK's air forces revealed for all to see, that in June 1952 the Air Ministry decided to order 25 examples of each aircraft, before either had flown. This must stand as one of the most nonsensical production decisions ever taken, for although each type was an excellent aircraft in its own right, and fully worthy of production as their subsequent histories have proved, the decision to produce two main V-bombers

(three with the inclusion of the Vickers Valiant) was patently wrong: three wholly different production lines had to be established, unit cost per aircraft was pushed up immeasurably by the small production runs, training was hampered, and stores holdings were increased considerably in terms of volume and administration. There can be no doubt that one type should have been selected for large-scale production, and history indicates that the Avro design would have been the best choice.

Be that as it may, both the H.P.80 and the Type 698 were ordered into small-scale production as the Handley-Page Victor and Avro Vulcan respectively. Both names were allocated within a month of the production contracts' issue.

The two prototype Vulcans (XW 777) in the lead fly in company with four Type 707 research aircraft. From top to bottom these are Types 707A, 707, 707C and 707A research machines.

Left: A Vulcan B.Mk 2A of No. 1 Group, RAF Strike Command, shows off the low-level camouflage of 1964 onwards. This scheme comprised dark green and medium sea grey (sometimes dark sea grey) above, and white or light grey below. From 1970 onwards the paint was gloss polyurethane, changing to matt finish in 1973, the year in which the original Type D roundels were superseded by Type B roundels without white rings. From 1979 the camouflage was extended over the radome.
Below: A Vulcan B.Mk 2A just after take-off reveals the geometry of the landing gear as it retracts, the strength of the main wheel doors being so great that no gear uplock is necessary.

Left: Visible on this Vulcan B.Mk 2A coming in to a landing are the highly effective airbrakes, with one below and two above each wing. In the fully extended position these multiplied drag by 250 per cent.

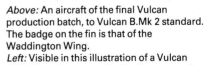

Above: An aircraft of the final Vulcan production batch, to Vulcan B.Mk 2 standard. The badge on the fin is that of the Waddington Wing.
Left: Visible in this illustration of a Vulcan B.Mk 2 are the retractable landing and taxiing lights (one under each wing) and the small blister under the nose for an optical bomb-aimer. This was not used in the Vulcan B.Mk 2 series.

A Vulcan B.Mk 2A of No. 101 Squadron (Waddington Wing) cruises above the clouds during a training flight in 1976.

Avro had built a number of test rigs to validate the engine system (three different types of engine being cleared initially for the Vulcan as a result of this effort), flight controls, electrical systems, hydraulic systems and fuel system, and this considerable effort in the early stage of the programme paid handsome dividends when the Woodford crew started on the assembly of the prototype, a task that proceeded with very few hitches. By the middle of August 1952 VX770 was complete, and immediately started its taxiing trials. It was ready at the end of the month for the first flight, an extremely successful excursion in the hands of Falk on 30 August. The only problem, and it was a relatively small one, was that the fairings for the main landing gear legs came off. As the aircraft was not intended for high-speed flights, this difficulty did not affect the test programme, which was resumed after VX770 had put in five appearances at the 1952 SBAC display in the company of the Types 707A and 707B. All were impressed with the striking delta-wing aircraft, VX770 being finished in white, the Type 707A in red and the Type 707B in blue, all with RAF markings. By the end of 1952 VX770 had amassed some 32 hours in the air, confirming the design team's initial predictions of handling and performance, and was then taken in hand for modification to approximate more closely to the production standard. The three main alterations were the installation of Armstrong Siddeley Sapphire ASSa.6 engines, each rated at 7,500-lb (3,402-kg) thrust, the installation of the wing fuel tanks, and the completion of the pressurization system. This last presented some difficulties, and it was not until July 1953 that VX770 was again able to participate in the test programme.

The second prototype, VX777, had been christened Vulcan in December 1952, and had since been completed to a more definitive standard. The engines were Bristol Olympus turbojets of the type selected for the production Vulcan: for ground tests Olympus Mk 99s were used, but before the second prototype first flew it was fitted with Olympus Mk 100 engines each rated at 9,750-lb (4,423-kg) thrust. The only noticeable external difference with this engine installation was the use of larger jetpipes. Apart from items of equipment relevant towards the development of an operational type, another difference was a lengthening of the fuselage by 16 in (40.64 m). As a result of tests with the Type 707B it had been decided to fit VX770 with a longer nosewheel leg to give the wings a ground incidence of 3½°, but this had necessitated the development of a telescoping leg to fit into the existing bay. This problem was removed in VX777, whose longer nosewheel bay could accommodate an untelescoping leg without difficulty; another benefit of the fuselage stretch was increased fuel capacity in the fuselage cells. Another visible alteration was the provision of a small blister on the underside of the forward fuselage to accommodate the visual bombing position.

VX777 was ready in time for a first flight on 3 September 1953, just before that year's SBAC show in the fashion that was becoming almost an Avro habit with the Type 698 and Type 707 series. Trials continued throughout the end of 1953 and beginning of 1954, the upper reaches of the speed and altitude envelopes being explored at the same time as a new engine control system was being proved. On 27 July 1954 VX777 was seriously damaged in a heavy landing, possibly as a result of the pilot letting speed drop too low at high angles of attack, a condition in which drag rises very sharply. The aircraft had virtually to be rebuilt, but this did permit the inclusion of a number of structural improvements resulting from tests with a static airframe. Another modification was the installation of Olympus Mk 101 engines, each rated at 11,000-lb (4,990-kg) thrust, with consequent improvements in performance right through the flight envelope but particularly at high altitude, where it was planned that the Vulcan should spend much of its operational life.

The Vulcan B.Mk 1

While prototype construction and testing was moving ahead, Avro was well under way with the first production series, in the form of 25 aircraft (XA889 to XA913) designated Avro Vulcan B.Mk 1. This variant was aerodynamically identical to the second Type 698 prototype but, as a result of flight trials and experience with the static test airframe and experimental rigs, included some 800 engineering changes to facilitate production at Woodford and also to produce a better aircraft. Externally, the only difference between the Vulcan B.Mk 1 and VX777 was the large nose radome, occupying the lower two-thirds of the nose section as far aft as the leading edge of the windscreen. This black 'electronically transparent' radome was composed of six layers of fibreglass and Hycar phenolic sponge, and was possibly the second largest aircraft radome in the world at the time. Inside this considerable radome lay the Vulcan's operational heart, namely the Navigation/Bombing System (H2S Mk 9A radar) and Navigation/Bombing Computer Mk 2, located just forward of the crew compartment. This accommodated the crew on two levels: at the higher level and facing forward were the pilot and co-pilot, seated under a jettisonable metal canopy on Martin-Baker Mk 3K or Mk 3KS ejector seats; and at the lower level and facing a large control panel on the rear bulkhead of the cabin were the navigator, radar operator and electronics officer, all on plain seats. The idea was that these three crewmen should in emergencies escape through the power-actuated ventral access door. Operational experience all too often revealed that this was insufficient, and the provision of rapid-inflation seat cushions (designed to push out the

The first squadron to receive Vulcan B.Mk 1s was No. 83 in 1957. Some of the squadron's aircraft are seen at Waddington.

Left: XH 504 was the 17th aircraft of the second production batch, and is seen as completed to Vulcan B.Mk 1 standard. The aircraft was later upgraded to Vulcan B.Mk 1A standard with a revised rear fuselage for a considerable ECM suite. Also well displayed is the stowed position for the airbrakes above the massive Phase 2 cranked wing.
Below: A Vulcan takes on fuel from a Valiant tanker at the rate of 500 Imp gal (2,273 litres) per minute during the early 1960s. The dark area aft of the port main gear leg is associated with the 'Green Satin' navigation radar.

XA 903 was the Vulcan B.Mk 1 used in the development trials for the Blue Steel stand-off nuclear missile.

occupant against high g-loads) did nothing to improve this inequitable situation. With hindsight it is possible to say that all five crewmen should have been provided with ejector seats right from the outset. The metal canopy over the pilot was fitted with two circular portholes, and there were also periscopes for rear vision.

XA889 made its first flight on 4 February 1955 with Olympus Mk 100 engines, but after only a few flights was fitted with the first definitive example of the Bristol engine, the Olympus Mk 101 rated at 11,000-lb (4,990-kg) thrust. There can be little doubt that this engine was one of the reasons for the Vulcan's great success over the years, for the Bristol team had in the BE.10/Olympus created one of the world's classic aero engines, which displayed sterling qualities of reliability while accepting modifications that saw a growth of power output unmatched in any other engine. This growth culminated in the afterburning Olympus 593 Mk 610, with a thrust rating of 38,050 lb (17,259 kg), a far cry indeed from the 9,000-lb

(4,082-kg) thrust anticipated by Chadwick when he started the design of the Type 698. The Vulcan was not fitted operationally with afterburning Olympus engines, but eventually flew operationally with Olympus marks offering well over double the power of these original units.

XA889 was delivered to Boscombe Down for service trials in March 1956, and at about the same time other Vulcan B.Mk 1 aircraft were delivered to other establishments as part of a combined manufacturer/service programme to push through as rapidly as possible to service deployment: XA890 was used for radar and radio trials, XA891 was operated for powerplant and fuel systems trials, and XA892 was flown for armament trials. The results of this intensive programme revealed few problems, and the Vulcan B.Mk 1 received its certificate of airworthiness on 29 May 1956.

The way was thus cleared for the Vulcan B.Mk 1 to enter service with the RAF, and the unit designated to phase the type into service was No. 230 Operational Conversion Unit, based at Waddington in Lincolnshire. XA895 and XA897 were allocated

to the unit in August 1956, but did not actually arrive at Waddington, instead staying at Boscombe Down for reliability trials. Thus it was not until January 1957 that No. 230 OCU finally received its first two aircraft, XA895 and XA898. Meanwhile XA897 had been lost in the most tragic circumstances: on 9 September 1956 the aircraft had departed from Boscombe Down on a goodwill visit to New Zealand, staging through Aden, Singapore and Melbourne. The trip was accomplished in record time and without incident until the very last moment: coming in to land at London Airport in poor conditions and under ground control, the aircraft hit the ground short of the runway, lurched into the air again and then crashed out of control. The two pilots (Squadron Leader Howard and Air Marshal Sir Harry Broadhurst, the Air Officer Commanding-in-Chief, RAF Bomber Command) escaped in their ejector seats, but the other four persons on board (three RAF officers and an Avro representative) could not escape through the ventral hatch and were killed.

With the arrival of its first aircraft, No. 230 OCU could begin the primary task of converting crews onto the new bomber. Most of these crews came from squadrons operating the English Electric Canberra twin-jet bomber, and their initial worries about the big delta-wing bomber were soon allayed: the lightly loaded aircraft handled with amazing agility and ease, and crews soon felt themselves completely at home. By the time the first conversion course ended on 20 May 1957, No. 230 OCU had seven Vulcans, though some of these had to be shared with the first operational Vulcan unit, No. 83 Squadron, also based at Waddington. This squadron formed with a nucleus of crews from the first conversion course, and was soon deeply involved in an intense working-up programme. No. 83 Squadron received its first aircraft, XA905, on 11 July 1957. The squadron had previously operated the Lincoln piston-engined bomber, while the second unit to form was previously equipped with Canberra B.Mk 6 light bombers, but was re-formed as a Vulcan unit at Finningley in Yorkshire on 15 October 1957. This unit, No. 101 Squadron, received its first Vulcan, XA909, on 17 October. The third unit to equip with the Vulcan B.Mk 1 was the celebrated No. 617 Squadron, which re-formed with Vulcans at Scampton in Lincolnshire on 1 May 1958. The squadron's first Vulcan was XH482, one of the follow-on batch of 37 Vulcans ordered from Avro's Woodford facility. The last aircraft of the original batch was XA913, which had been delivered on 19 December 1957.

Of this total of 62 aircraft ordered as Vulcan B.Mk 1s, only 45 were in fact completed as such, the last Vulcan B.Mk 1 being delivered on 30 April 1959. The balance of the second order (from XH533 onwards) was completed to a much improved standard. Within this group of 45 Vulcan B.Mk 1s, moreover, there was a subdivision into two variants, the original Vulcan B.Mk 1 and the improved

Avro Vulcan B.Mk 1A, the latter featuring a revised and bulbous rear fuselage fitted with a comprehensive ECM (electronic countermeasures) suite. This was intended as a complete package, and could be retrofitted on the Handley Page Victor. Of the first 20 production Vulcans XA900, XA901, XA904, XA906, XA907 and XA909 to XA913 (10 aircraft) were modified to Vulcan B.Mk 1A standard, and the 20 initial-standard aircraft of the second batch (XH475 to XH483, XH497 to XH506, and XH532) were completed as Vulcan B.Mk 1As.

While this modification did much to improve the Vulcan's defensive capability, overall improvement in performance was being achieved by the installation of uprated engines, the Olympus Mk 101 being replaced first by the Olympus Mk 102 rated at 12,000-lb (5,443-kg) thrust and then by the definitive Vulcan B.Mk 1/1A engine, the Olympus Mk 104 rated at 13,400-lb (6,078-kg) thrust.

Another modification approved in the later 1950s, after extensive trials in 1958, was the provision of an inflight-refuelling system provided by Flight Refuelling Ltd. The necessary plumbing for such a capability had been installed right from the beginning of production, but it was only late in the decade that the probe (mounted on top of the nose on the centreline above the radar installation) was fitted and certified for service use. Interestingly enough, the normal refuelling facilities in the main landing gear wells could handle only 150 Imp gal (682 litres) per minute, whereas the nose probe was initially cleared for 500 Imp gal (2,273 litres) and later 1,000 Imp gal (4,546 litres) per minute. Flight Refuelling also developed a 'buddy' refuelling system for the Vulcan, comprising a kit that could be installed in the weapons bay: this kit comprised a 5,000-Imp gal (22,730-litre) tank of transfer fuel and a hose-reel unit that could stream a drogue-fitted

receptacle for the probe of a thirsty Vulcan.

It is worth noting at this point that most of these Vulcan B.Mk 1/1A aircraft had lost the virtually pure triangular wing of the prototypes, for continued research into the problems that might be encountered in high-speed flight, undertaken by the Type 707A and by prototype VX770, had revealed that the Vulcan's performance was such that it was likely to encounter the same type of high-speed buffet that had already beset fighter aircraft. It was soon appreciated that such buffet could seriously affect the fatigue life of the wing structure. Fortunately, however, experience with fighters and in the wind tunnel had already provided the solution: the extension of chord on the outboard section of the wings, combined with the drooping and thinning of the leading edge over this extended-chord portion of the wing.

The result of this realization was first flown in the modified Type 707A, and the fully defined Phase 2 wing was proved after the prototype VX777 took to the air again on 5 September 1955 after modification between July and September of that year. The Phase 2 wing completely altered the shape of the Vulcan's wing, for it introduced a cranked leading edge: from the root to 48.5 per cent semi-span leading edge sweep was 52°, reducing to 42° sweep to 78 per cent semi-span, and then increasing again to 52° sweep out to a tip that was increased fairly considerably in chord. This gave a forward crank to the intermediate portion of each wing, and this local chord extension of about 20 per cent was thinned and drooped to produce a type of conical camber that usefully pushed back the buffet threshold. Avro also thought that a row of vortex generators would usefully speed the boundary layer above the wing and mitigate the problem. Thus several Vulcans were flown with rows of 19 such

Above: A Vulcan B.Mk 2 lifts off the runway of an RAF operational airfield. Thanks to the provision of compressed-air starters, all four engines could be started together, permitting the aircraft to begin rolling after two minutes and airborne two minutes after that. This was of particular importance given the short warning time that would have been given of any Soviet missile attack against V-bomber bases.

Right: The Vulcan B.Mk 2 series had a revised control-surface arrangement with elevons (outer and inner pairs) on each wing, as indicated by the deflections along the trailing edge of this Vulcan B.Mk 2.

In its Mk 2 form amply endowed with power, the Vulcan possessed very good take-off performance and climb.

generators located at 25 per cent chord on each wing behind the kink; inboard of the kink the generators were spaced 22.5 in (57.15 cm) apart, and outboard of the kink 11.25 in (28.575 cm) apart. It was soon discovered, however, that the cranked wing rendered these generators superfluous and they were thus removed. The

development of the Phase 2 wing, it should be noted, was sufficiently rapid that all but a few (possibly the first five) Vulcan B.Mk 1s were built without it, some of these aircraft not receiving it even as a retrofit.

Although developed by Avro as prototype installations, the Mach trimmer and yaw/pitch dampers that formed the autostabilization system used even on the earliest production Vulcans were built by Louis Newmark, specialists in such

equipment. The Mach trimmer gradually deflected the elevators upwards with increasing speed to counter the rearward shift in the centre of pressure with increases in Mach number, and the yaw and pitch dampers were advanced units incorporating rate and position feedback systems. This autostabilization system reached an early peak of perfection by June 1956, and was thus available for production aircraft from an early date.

The Vulcan B.Mk 2

Long before the first Vulcans began to enter service, Avro had started work on a much improved version of the basic aircraft, made possible and indeed inevitable by the extraordinary growth in the power delivered by improved variants of the Olympus engine, most notably the Olympus BO1.6 series under development in the mid-1950s with thrust ratings envisaged in the order of 16,000 lb (7,258 kg). As the operational philosophy of the time called for extra altitude and extra speed wherever possible, the extra power of the Olympus BO1.6 series was seen as making possible such advances in the Vulcan. From the designers' point of view, however, this increase in ceiling and speed had the effect of

dropping the Vulcan straight back into the buffet problem from which the cranked wing had rescued it at lower speed and lower altitude. What was needed, therefore, was a wing with greater outboard area but lower thickness/chord ratio.

The result was the Phase 4 wing, which Avro submitted to the Air Ministry in September 1955 for criticism. Approval was forthcoming immediately, at least in terms of encouragement if not of contracts, so Avro decided to press ahead with what might well be called a second-generation derivative of the basic design. The design teams were hard at work by the end of the year, and in March 1956 the Air Ministry sanctioned the building of a prototype wing, though this was to be installed on

the initial second prototype, VX777, rather than on a new aircraft. In April 1956 the Air Ministry contracted for production of a revised bomber with the Phase 4 wing, to be designated Avro Vulcan B.Mk 2. This new model would clearly offer considerably greater operational capability than the Vulcan B.Mk 1 series, and it was decided at this time to end production of the initial series at 45 aircraft, the last 17 of the second production order being reinstated as the first of what was ultimately 89 Vulcan B.Mk 2 series aircraft.

The most notable external difference between the Vulcan B.Mk 1 and the Vulcan B.Mk 2 was naturally the Phase 4 wing: this spanned 12 ft (3.66 m) more than the wing of the Vulcan B.Mk 1 series and was of considerably reduced thickness/chord ratio. Apart from mitigating the buffet

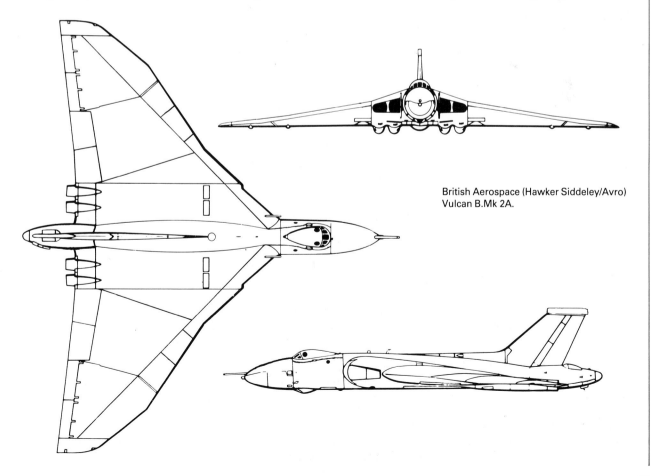

British Aerospace (Hawker Siddeley/Avro) Vulcan B.Mk 2A.

problem, the greater area of the wing also bestowed increased ceiling on the Vulcan B.Mk 2 series. There were also another 90 or so major modifications between the Vulcan B.Mk 1 and Vulcan B.Mk 2, but space precludes mention of all but the most important of these. Firstly, the inlet ducts were enlarged to make possible a mass flow of some 700 lb (317.5 kg) per second at sea level; this was necessary to provide the Olympus BO1.6 series with adequate air, and was also designed to permit further increases in demand from more powerful engines. Secondly, the jetpipes were also enlarged to cater for the new powerplant's greater demands, with potential for further growth; at the same time steel rings were built into the jetpipe structure to cater for carry-through loads associated with the rear spar. Thirdly, the airframe was completely restressed to cater for maximum take-off weights in excess of 200,000 lb (90,720 kg); this restressing allowed the carriage of more fuel, extending the Vulcan B.Mk 2's range quite considerably. Fourthly, and associated with the third change, the landing gear was also restressed and redesigned to cater for the increased maximum take-off weight; the nosewheel leg was shortened, and the main legs were redesigned although the bogies and levered suspension were unaltered. Fifthly, an auxiliary power unit (Rover 2S/150 gas turbine) was built into the starboard wing aft of the landing gear hinge to provide emergency power supplies in the air. Sixthly, the electrical system was completely changed, the original 112-volt DC system being replaced by a 200-volt AC system based on

four parallel constant-speed drive and generators to provide greater capacity. And seventhly, the flight controls were altered completely to comprise inner and outer elevons on each wing, each being divided into two portions with independent and totally separate power units.

As may be imagined, this was an enormous undertaking at a time when the company was busy producing the first production aircraft for the RAF, and an indication of the importance attached to the programme is provided by the fact that no less than 13 of the first 16 Vulcans were allocated to the test programme, together with two later aircraft further on into the effort. One of the early aircraft was, of course, VX777, which was rebuilt with the Phase 4 wing and its controls from August 1956. In its revised form VX777 first flew on 31 August 1957, and although it had the revised inlets it retained the Olympus Mk 102 engines. Other Vulcan B.Mk 1s used in the programme were XA890 (avionics development), XA891 (powerplant development),

XA892 (weapons development), XA893 (electrical systems development), XA894 (other systems development), XA899 (avionics development) and XA903 (development of and interface with the Avro Blue Steel stand-off missile). This last weapon was to become the main nuclear weapon of the Vulcan B.Mk 2 series (see below), and all Vulcan B.Mk 2 aircraft had provision for Blue Steel-related equipment, though this was in fact fitted only to later production aircraft.

Such was the importance of this second-generation bomber that Avro bent all its energies into as

XA 903 departs for Woomera in Australia for full-range trials with the unarmed Blue Steel missile.

rapid a development as possible, and the first Vulcan B.Mk 2 (XH533) flew on 19 August 1958, some eight months before the last Vulcan B.Mk 1A. However, this and some of the next production Vulcan B.Mk 2s were hybrid types, retaining the original Vulcan B.Mk 1 tailcones without ECM gear, and lacking several typical Vulcan B.Mk 2 features amongst their systems. To this extent, therefore, the second Vulcan B.Mk 2 (XH534) may be regarded

Left: A Blue Steel-equipped Vulcan B.Mk 2 comes in to land. Note the unused visual bombing blister and the large radome for the H2S Mk 9A bombing radar.
Right: The after bulkhead of the bomb bay accommodated the jacks and their 'plumbing' for the actuation of the doors.

as the first production aircraft to the revised standard. It too lacked some items of Vulcan B.Mk 2 standard equipment, but had 17,000-lb (7,711-kg) thrust Olympus BO1.6 Mk 201 engines in place of XH533's 16,000-lb (7,258-kg) thrust Olympus BO1.6 Mk 200 engines, the ECM-fitted bulged rear fuselage, and an additional ECM platform between the jetpipes of the engines on the starboard side of the aircraft with a flush aerial on the undersurface of the wing. Provision was made for a comparable unit on the port side of the aircraft, but this was never needed. This aircraft first flew in January 1959, and was considerably more representative of the definitive Vulcan B.Mk 2 than XH533.

Mention has been made above of the Blue Steel stand-off missile. This impressive weapon, developed by Avro's Weapon Research Division, also based at Woodford, started life in 1954 with the realization that the development of surface-to-air missiles would eventually prevent manned bombers from penetrating deep into enemy air space at high level for the free-fall delivery of nuclear weapons onto primary targets that

would almost inevitably be ringed by the most capable surface-to-air missiles. The stand-off missile offered a solution to this problem, for the launch aircraft would not need to penetrate as deeply into enemy air space, and could yet deliver an equally devastating warhead over a considerable range with even less chance of destruction than before. Design of the Blue Steel began in 1954, and the Vulcan was clearly an ideal launch platform as the underside of the fuselage with its massive weapon bay could relatively easily be converted to carry one Blue Steel in a semi-recessed position. Avro was convinced that the Vulcan B.Mk 1A could have been operational with the Blue Steel by 1959, but political vacillation, deriving largely from financial problems, meant that it was 1959 before the definitive Blue Steel with the Stentor liquid-propellant rocket was available for trials. Much of the development work with the Blue Steel was carried out by a Vulcan B.Mk 1 (XA903), though the final trials and operational development tasks were entrusted to a pair of Vulcan B.Mk 2s (XH538 and XH539), which fired the weapon (without

XH 537 was one of two Vulcan B.Mk 2s fitted with the Avro-designed pylons for underwing carriage of the Skybolt.

warhead) at the Weapons Research Establishment at Woomera in Australia. The Blue Steel was thus operational only with Vulcan B.Mk 2 squadrons, and then only for a short time before the British nuclear deterrent, as it was now styled, was switched to the Royal Navy's force of four nuclear-powered submarines each with 16 Lockheed Polaris missiles.

The first seven Vulcan B.Mk 2s off the production line were all used for the development programme of the type undertaken at Boscombe Down, though of these aircraft (XH533 to XH539) four later reached operational squadrons after being brought up to full Vulcan B.Mk 2 standard. Thus the first aircraft of the mark to reach the RAF proper was XH558 (the 12th aircraft), which was handed over to No. 230 Operational Conversion Unit on 1 July 1960. The first Vulcan B.Mk 2 to enter squadron service was XH554, which reached No. 83 Squadron on 23 December 1960.

Deliveries gathered pace in

1960, all production aircraft by this time having 17,000-lb (7,711-kg) Olympus BO1.6 Mk 201 engines. By 1961 it was abundantly clear that if the Vulcans were to remain credible as the platforms for the UK's deterrent they would have to be able to scramble more quickly, for Soviet missiles would otherwise destroy them on the ground. The solution to this need was relatively straightforward, the original Rotax electric starters for the engines being replaced by a compressed-

The Skybolt was a most attractive weapon option for the Vulcan, which with the proposed Phase 6 wing could have carried six such missiles.

air starter and a cross-bleed system by which any engine could be started from any other, permitting the simultaneous start of all four engines, roll two minutes after engine start and take-off two minutes later. This starter system had been developed for the Olympus Mk 301, and when fitted to the Olympus Mk 201 engine in Vulcan B.Mk 2s produced an engine designated Olympus Mk 202. The Olympus Mk 301 already mentioned was the ultimate production engine used in the Vulcan series, and became available in 1963. This magnificent engine was rated at 20,000-lb

(9,072-kg) thrust thanks to the addition of a zero stage on the low-pressure compressor, resulting in a virtual doubling of the engine's mass-flow capability in comparison with the Olympus Mk 100 available only five years earlier. When fitted with this engine the Vulcan B.Mk 2 became the Avro Vulcan B.Mk 2A, and though maximum low-altitude power could not be used except at take-off for fear of exceeding airframe limitations, the availability of this extra power did much to perk up the Vulcan B.Mk 2A's medium- and high-altitude climb performance and

ceiling.

While the Blue Steel missile was undergoing its final stages of development in the later 1950s, the British government had been considering the future requirements of the UK nuclear deterrent force, and in March 1960 it was decided that while progress was being made with a British-developed land-based strategic missile, the Blue Streak, greater capability could be obtained for less cost by the purchase of an American air-launched missile. The AGM-87A Skybolt was lighter than the comparable Blue Steel (11,500 lb/5,216 kg in comparison with

15,000 lb/6,804 kg) and also slimmer, making it possible to carry a substantial number of such weapons on underwing pylons. The aircraft manufacturers had not been consulted in any way before the decision was taken by the government, and so rapid calculations were the order of the day as Avro and Handley Page sought to show that their aircraft could carry more Skybolts. Avro could demonstrate that underwing installations for two or four missiles were immediately possible, with considerable growth potential available for further missiles, and the Air Ministry decided to cut back production of the Victor in light of this 'force multiplying' show by Avro. The decision was short-sighted in the

extreme, and was one of the nails in the coffin of Handley Page, whose financial difficulties were becoming acute.

As part of the development programme before introduction of the Skybolt to the British inventory, three Vulcans were allocated to aerodynamic, structural, systems and compatibility trials with the American weapon: these were all Vulcan B.Mk 2s, XH563 being sent to California for electronic compatibility trials at the Douglas facility of Santa Monica, where the Skybolt was being produced, while XH537 and XH538 were fitted with Avro-designed underwing pylons and sent to Florida for launch and separation trials with the new missile. The whole programme was undertaken with great speed

A Vulcan B.Mk 2 streams off the runway of a British airfield.

and complete success, but then a new American President, John F. Kennedy, cancelled the whole Skybolt programme.

The British government now saw fit to recast the entire UK nuclear strategy, the service responsible for the deterrent force thus becoming the Royal Navy with Polaris missiles bought from the USA. While this force was being readied, the Royal Air Force was to soldier on in the role, the primary weapon being the Blue Steel missile which finally became operational with No. 617 Squadron in February 1963.

It is interesting to speculate what might have happened had not the Americans cancelled the Skybolt, for Avro had been working on a highly advanced version of the Vulcan B.Mk 2 to offer maximum utility with the Skybolt. This machine, which would have entered service as the Vulcan B.Mk 3, was designed round the Phase 6 wing and uprated engines. The Phase 6 wing saw a return towards the more conventional delta shape, though with span increased to 117 ft 6 in (35.81 m);

the powerplant was to have consisted of four 22,500-lb (10,206-kg) Olympus 23 engines fed from integral wing tankage which, as it distributed fuel loads throughout the wing (rather than close to the centreline as on existing marks) permitted a structure weight little increased over that of the Phase 4 wing despite the increased fuel load and maximum take-off weight being increased to 350,000 lb (158,760 kg). The revised aircraft could have carried six Skybolts (a load of 69,000 lb/31,298 kg) externally, or a combined internal and external load of 38 1,000-lb (454-kg) conventional bombs, arranged 3-4-3 in the bomb bay and tandem 2-3-2 in twin pods suspended from the middle Skybolt hardpoints under each wing. Maximum range was calculated as 5,750 miles (9,253 km), and seven-hour missions were anticipated. This Vulcan B.Mk 3 would have been a truly great warplane, and would have met the subsequent (but unforeseen) needs of the Royal Air Force far better than the Vulcan B.Mk 2 series.

A No. 101 Squadron Vulcan B.Mk 2A lifts off from Nellis AFB during a 'Red Flag' exercise in the USA.

While this political and strategic manoeuvring was raising and then dashing hopes in Avro and the Royal Air Force, the latter had been reaching the inevitable conclusion that the high-level role for which the Vulcan had been conceived was no longer operationally feasible given the capabilities of the Soviet manned interceptor and surface-to-air missile defences. Thus from the middle of 1963 the Vulcan force was redeployed to the low-level penetration role, in the hope that the bombers could sneak into enemy airspace below the edge of radar cover to deliver their weapons, at first the Blue Steel missile (which was for some inexplicable reason phased out of service almost as soon as it entered service in the mid-1960s) and then a 'conventional' load comprising a maximum of 21 1,000-lb (454-kg) free-fall bombs.

Previous pages: At low level the Vulcan was always an impressive sight (and sound), as may be imagined from this illustration of four Vulcan B.Mk 2As. The rearmost aircraft (XM 597) was the first to be fitted with the radar warning receiver at the top of the fin. *Above:* A Vulcan B.Mk 2 releases its load of 1,000-lb (454-kg) HE bombs at high altitude.

Above: A Vulcan B.Mk 2 lines itself up for a low-level pass during an air display in West Germany during 1974. Vulcans were never based in West Germany.
Inset above: The pimple below the probe on the nose of this Vulcan B.Mk 2 houses the antenna for the terrain-following radar.

With this change to the low-level role, the all-white finish of the Vulcans was rapidly changed to conventional camouflage of dark green and medium (sometimes dark) sea grey above, with white (sometimes light aircraft grey) below, relieved only by RAF markings, serial numbers, lettered instructions, occasional squadron markings, and black on the radome and dielectric panels. To reduce the chances of overall destruction by Soviet missiles, the Vulcans were generally dispersed as groups of four to as many 'Bomber Country' airfields as possible, this being made more effective by the reorganization of Vulcan servicing to a central depot from the previous wing organization.

Apart from the camouflage, another feature that distinguished these low-level Vulcans was the pimple radome added to the extreme nose; this contained the antenna for the terrain-following radar whose effectiveness was proved in a series of trials conducted over Cyprus in 1966.

Not visible externally was another important modification, namely a buffet meter to monitor fatigue conditions in the Vulcan's large wing, which was totally unsuited to the high-gust low-level role as a result of its considerable area and span, the two features specifically developed to make possible sustained high-altitude flight. Yet such was the greatness of the basic design that the Vulcan was able to operate in this markedly revised role, though the resultant operational value of the expensive Vulcan squadrons was at best problematical: it is hard to see that any of these massive aircraft could have penetrated far into the

A pair of Vulcan B.Mk 2s sails sedately past the early warning radar station at Fylingdales in the county of Yorkshire. In time of war such a facility would have given Bomber Command (later Strike Command) time to scramble its V-bombers.

airspace of a sophisticated foe even at night or in adverse weather. Even if the aircraft had succeeded, moreover, the 21,000-lb (9,526-kg) load of conventional (not even guided or 'smart') munitions was not notably larger than that which could be carried by the single- and twin-engine strike aircraft that were beginning to enter European and American service during this period. Perhaps the Vulcan B.Mk 2A's greatest asset was the ever-developing ECM suite, still largely classified, though the most notable was the ARI.18228 passive ECM system, with its antennae in a rectangular pod located at the top of the vertical tail surfaces in a most distinctive installation. Other systems included items for the recording, analysing and jamming of hostile radars, deception jammers and chaff launchers.

With the last Vulcan B.Mk 2A delivered in 1964, the Vulcan B.Mk 1A disappeared from service quite rapidly. Some aircraft were scrapped, others became instructional airframes at various RAF bases and other establishments, and four became engine test-beds. These aircraft were XV770, delivered to Rolls-Royce at Langar for trials with the Rolls-Royce RCo.5 Conway turbofan; XA902 used for trials with the Conway 11 and Rolls-Royce Spey; XA894 used for trials with the Olympus 22R mounted in a ventral package as part of the development programme for the BAC TSR.2; and XA903 used for trials with the Olympus 593 in a ventral package as part of the development programme for the Aerospatiale/BAC Concorde supersonic airliner.

The Ultimate Developments

By the late 1960s the V-bomber force had gone into decline, evidence of this among the Vulcan units being the disbandment of Nos 12 and 83 Squadrons in 1967 and 1969 respectively. At the same time the Vulcans' increasing relegation to a secondary role was evidenced by the transfer of Nos 9 and 35 Squadrons to Akrotiri in Cyprus in 1969 as the two bomber units of the Near East Air Force Bomber Wing.

Yet there was life left in the Vulcan yet, as indicated by the re-forming of No. 27 Squadron in 1973 with a complement of four Avro Vulcan SR.Mk 2A aircraft, which was alternatively designated Avro Vulcan B.Mk 2 (MRR). This squadron was entrusted with the radar surveillance of sea areas of interest to the UK, and its aircraft were fitted with classified sensor systems (electronic, optical and other) and increased fuel capacity. The squadron was disbanded in March 1982, the four modified Vulcans being handed over to No. 44 Squadron which flew in the maritime reconnaissance role for a further few weeks.

What finally spelled the end for the now-venerable Vulcan was the service appearance of the Panavia Tornado two-seat variable-geometry interdictor and strike aircraft. This replaced the Vulcan in the overland role, and financial difficulties made it uneconomic to revise the Vulcans' airframes for increased fatigue life in the overwater role that had up to that time been considered for the type. Early in 1981, therefore, it was decided to disband all the remaining Vulcan squadrons between June 1981 and June 1982 as the Tornado began to enter widespread service. This disbandment programme was well under way (No. 230 OCU, and Nos 617, 35, 27 and 9 Squadrons had gone between August 1981 and April 1982) when the Argentine invasion of the Falkland Islands finally gave the Vulcan its last chance, for the type was the only aircraft with the range/

A Vulcan SR.Mk 2 of No. 27 Squadron from RAF Scampton flies over an oil platform during a North Sea patrol.

payload capability to operate with the aid of inflight-refuelling from Wideawake on Ascension Island for raids against targets in the Falkland Islands. Only Nos 44, 50 and 101 Squadrons were still operational with the Vulcan, and their disbandment was well under way. No. 44 Squadron was charged with support of the South Atlantic Task Force, and one Vulcan SR.Mk 2A was dispatched to Ascension Island while a few other Vulcan B.Mk 2A bombers were put into full operational order. The Vulcan SR.Mk 2A flew radar reconnaissance to South Georgia Island with the aid of inflight-refuelling, and the scene was then set for the Vulcans' only combat sorties. A small detachment of bombers arrived at Wideawake Air Base in the closing days of April 1982, and on 30 April

the first attack was flown. One aircraft left Ascension with a load of 14 1,000-lb (454 kg) bombs and, after inflight-refuelling from a Victor K.Mk 2 tanker, arrived over Port Stanley airfield at 04.30 on the morning of 1 May, flying obliquely at 35° over the runway to unload its stick from 25,000 ft (7,620 m). One bomb damaged the edge of the runway, and the Vulcan B.Mk 2A then turned for home, arriving at Wideawake after a flight of more than 8,000 miles (12,875 km), the longest combat sortie ever flown. Further sorties were flown (some with AGM-45A Shrike anti-radiation missiles) but no further bombs were dropped.

While these combat sorties were being flown, the British Aerospace Manchester Division had been improvising the ultimate Vulcan variant, the Avro Vulcan

K.Mk 2 inflight-refuelling tanker. The Falklands operation had revealed a great shortfall in the Royal Air Force's inflight-refuelling capability, and the existing Vulcan airframes were seen as a means of remedying this deficiency quickly: a hosereel unit was located in the erstwhile ECM bay in the tailcone, and transfer fuel was provided in a tank located in the weapons bay. The first conversion flew on 18 June 1982, and the type was cleared for service on 23 June. Six conversions were completed, but they were too late to see service in the Falklands operation. However, the aircraft remained in service until the end of 1983 and were the final operational versions of the once powerful Vulcan nuclear bomber.

Specifications

Vulcan B. Mk1 & Mk1A

Type:	long-range strategic bomber
Accommodation:	5 on flight deck
Armament:	up to 21,000 lbs (9,526 kg) of conventional or nuclear bombs
Powerplant:	four 13,000-lb (5,897-kg) thrust Bristol Olympus Mk 104 turbojets
Performance:	
maximum Speed	about 625 mph (1,006 km/h) or Mach 0.95 at 40,000 ft (12,192 m)
cruising speed	about 600 mph (966 km/h)
initial climb rate	—
service ceiling	above 50,000 ft (15,240 m)
range	3,000 miles (4,825 km)
Weights:	
empty equipped	—
normal take-off	160,000 lbs (72,567 kg)
maximum take-off	200,000 lbs (90,720 kg)
Dimensions:	
span	99 ft (30.18 m)
length	97 ft 1 in (29.59 m)
height	26 ft 6 in (8.08 m)
wing area	3,554 sq ft (330.17 m²)

Vulcan B. Mk2 & Mk2A

Type:	long-range strategic bomber
Accommodation:	5 on flight deck
Armament:	up to 21,000 lbs (9,526 kg) of conventional or nuclear bombs
Powerplant:	four 20,000-lb (9,072-kg) thrust Bristol Olympus Mk 301 turbojets
Performance:	
maximum Speed	645 mph (1,038 km/h) at high altitude
cruising speed	625 mph (1,005 km/h) at 50,000 ft (15,240 m)
initial climb rate	—
service ceiling	55,000 ft (16,765 m)
range	2,300 miles (3,700 km)
Weights:	
empty equipped	—
normal take-off	—
maximum take-off	more than 200,000 lbs (90,720 kg)
Dimensions:	
span	111 ft (33.83 m)
length	100 ft 1 in (30.50 m)
height	27 ft 2 in (8.29 m)
wing area	3,964 sq ft (368.3 m²)

We would particularly like to thank Mr Harry Holmes of British Aerospace Aircraft Group, for his invaluable help with illustrations for this publication.

Picture research was through Military Archive & Research Services, Braceborough, Lincolnshire and unless otherwise indicated below all material was supplied by British Aerospace.

Austin Brown – 10 (centre & bottom), 17, 19, 20 (top & bottom), 21 (top & bottom), 22 (bottom), 25, 34 (top), 39, 41.

Crown Copyright (MOD-RAF) – 2-3, 10 (top), 11, 14, 18, 20-21, 22 (top), 23, 24 (bottom), 34 (bottom), 36-37, 42, 49-53 (top), 54-55.

Flight International – 6-7.

Military Archive & Research Services – 35 (top & bottom), 53 (bottom).